A Festering Sweetness

A delirium of solutions, forthwith, forces
him into back streets, to begin again:
up hollow stairs among acrid smells
to obscene rendezvous. And there he finds
a festering sweetness of red lollipops—
and a yelping dog.

William Carlos Williams,
Paterson I

A festering

Sweetness

POEMS OF AMERICAN PEOPLE

ROBERT COLES

UNIVERSITY OF

PITTSBURGH PRESS

Published by the University of Pittsburgh Press, Pittsburgh, Pa. 15260
Copyright © 1978, Robert Coles
All rights reserved
Feffer and Simons, Inc., London
Manufactured in the United States of America

Library of Congress Cataloging in Publication Data

Coles, Robert.
    A festering sweetness.

    (Pitt poetry series)
    1. Poor—United States—Poetry. I. Title.
PS3553.047456F4   811'.5'4   77–15736
ISBN 0–8229–3371–3
ISBN 0–8229–5290–4 pbk.

Grateful acknowledgment is here made to the Estate of Florence H.
Williams for permission to reprint lines from Paterson, copyright 1946
by W. C. Williams; and an excerpt of a previously unpublished letter
by William Carlos Williams, copyright 1978 by the Estate of Florence H.
Williams. Published by permission of New Directions.

Publication of this book

was made possible

by a grant from the

Maurice Falk Medical Fund,

Pittsburgh, Pennsylvania.

To the men, women, and children who speak in this book—and to others like them, who live in various parts of the United States of America. And, again, to the memory of William Carlos Williams.

CONTENTS

PREFACE

his particular volume of words, images, thoughts,
observations, fragments of ideas and feelings requires
a bit of explanation. Since 1958—that is, for some
twenty years now—I have been working with a fairly
broad range of American children. I started my work a
rather smug and all too self-satisfied child psychiatrist,
just out of medical training and in the Air Force
as a physician. It happened that I was stationed at
Keesler Air Force Base in Biloxi, Mississippi, when
the civil rights movement spread across the South. I
witnessed a "swim-in" along the Gulf of Mexico, right
outside my home—and on Sunday, no less, upon
returning from church. I witnessed the growing violence
in New Orleans as the day of court-ordered desegre-
gation approached. Rather than return to my native
New England I decided to remain in the South. I
decided to try to find out how children who come face
to face with a serious social and political crisis manage
to get along psychologically—manage, really, to
initiate (in the course of their everyday lives) what
others call a moment of historical change.

Eventually, my sense of what I hoped to accomplish
began to change. I had started out with psychiatric
questions—how do particular boys or girls deal with a
serious social stress?—but I soon realized that I was
meeting families whose assumptions, hopes, fears, and
expectations were quite definitely strange to me. I
realized, too, how arbitrarily I was fitting the lives of
various individuals into my psychiatric categories—a

useful practice under certain circumstances, but now, for me, a distinct hindrance. I was unwittingly setting severe, maybe crippling, limits on what I would allow myself to see, try to comprehend. Always it was the trouble I sought out—evidence of anxiety, fear, anger, envy, jealousy; or the denial of those emotions; or their projection on others; and so forth. It took a six-year-old black child, daily facing heckling and threatening mobs outside a virtually abandoned school building, to bring me (a little bit, at least) to my senses: "I don't worry, no sir, I don't. I just go ahead past the crowd of people. They're the ones who are worried—about me. I'm only worried about them, not myself. I'm not screaming and shouting. I'm not calling people bad names. They must have bad dreams when they go to bed. When I go to bed, I say my prayers with my grandmother, and she tells me how lucky I am, and the next thing, its morning, and I wake up feeling real good. I'm ready to put on my wings and fly. I'm ready to wax the sidewalks and slide, slide to school. I'm ready to be nice to those people; the worse their names for me, the bigger the smile—the sun in my face breaking through the rain clouds in theirs, and getting where it wants to be."

She went on, later, to offer other images: a vine, growing and growing, even along a dark side of the house; a kite, dragging along the ground, going nowhere at all, but suddenly getting caught by the wind and rising higher and higher. I listened, talked with her, played games with her, asked her to draw pictures, did a few myself, and began to see that this lively, imaginative child had in various ways all along been telling me to go ply my trade elsewhere. Yes, there were plenty of clouds to be examined; but she was, indeed, a sun of sorts—warm, a central figure to her people, a cause of their growth. She had penetrated a prevailing climate of opinion, buttressed by laws, and had become a pioneer in the struggle for desegregated schools. She had shown herself able to overcome various obstacles, assert herself, and rise to an occasion, however sad and difficult. Why wasn't I inclined to study that psychological process, if not outright triumph? she wondered in her own polite, self-effacing way. And why, too, didn't I heed what she *did* say, from time to time, rather than always come back with those dreary, somewhat heavy-handed, and increasingly predictable inquiries she had learned to accept as an unfortunate measure of me?

Eventually, she and other children taught me to relax a little; sit and draw with them—without suggesting "topics"; simply talk, or watch television, or discuss "nothing special" or "anything that pops up," a specification of sorts once handed down to me as an appropriate substitute for the interview of a field worker. Eventually, I abandoned a carefully rehearsed agenda and responded to *her*, to the verbal or artistic initiatives of her rather spunky spirit. And there were others I got to meet, others whose voices I have with me on

stacks of tapes, others whose faces I sometimes see
when I close my eyes and wonder where the time has
gone: black youth from the rural South; sons and
daughters of sharecroppers and tenant farmers; white
Southern children; boys and girls whose parents are
farm workers; the young of Appalachia's hollows;
ghetto children; young Indians, Eskimos, and Chicanos,
who live out West or in Alaska; or the sons and
daughters of American factory workers. In five volumes
of *Children of Crisis,* I have spelled out more pre-
cisely—and at greater length, indeed—exactly which
children, and where they have lived and how I have
come to know them, and what they have wanted (so
very much) and tried hard to teach me.

Here I want to say something else—how the poems,
the words and images and fragments of expression,
came together in this volume. Years ago, before I went
South, I got to know William Carlos Williams, whom
I wrote about as an undergraduate. (I have spelled out,
in *William Carlos Williams: The Knack of Survival in
America,* the details of a much treasured acquaintance.)
He took me once on his medical rounds and later wrote
me a note, part of which said this: "Every day I hear
those poor souls I visit talk poems to me. Sometimes I
run to my car and write a few of their words down. Not
every day, but on a lucky day, two or three times.
Don't tell your Harvard professor what I said!"

He was being unnecessarily defensive and truculent.
He was *not* romanticizing his working-class patients,

whom he both loved and disliked, needed and resented.
He could not live with them, could not live without
them. He applauded them, took heartily to their robust,
hard-laboring life, knew many of them to be utterly
decent and thoughtful and kind—but also saw the scars,
the warts, the mean and callous and hurt and sad
side of their condition, the mix he referred to once
as a "festering sweetness." They fed his writing but
also kept him from it or, rather, gave him to it tired and
a touch embittered. In his letter he was describing
what he heard, from day to day, in the hope that an
aspiring doctor would not feel completely removed in
future years from the moments of poetry in everyday
life. In *Paterson*, of course, and in the stories collected
as *Life Along the Passaic River*, he collected those
moments and much more—wedded them to the marve-
lous sensibility and literary skills of a poet, a novelist.
"Raw diamonds," he once said to me, after we'd both
left a tenement house in a northern New Jersey industrial
town. He had in mind a few seconds of eloquence—a
mother's philosophical why's as she watched her girl
die and heard the doctor say there was nothing more
he could do. He had plenty of sharpness in him to grind
away at words; and he could polish things rather
bright too. Late at night, tired but all heated up, almost
agitated, his mind sifted, used, discarded.

Lacking such gifts, I can only offer a few high marks
in a wandering doctor-observer's work with American
children, who, it turns out, have (so often) spoken

with more candor and lucidity and imagination and
verve than all too many grown-ups manage (including,
alas, not a few social scientists). Over the years I have
found myself, at certain moments, quite struck by the
observations of certain boys or girls, put to me in
unforgettable words. These have not been children
making a conscious effort to write or trying to please
a teacher. Sometimes they have been children talking
to other children. Sometimes they have been children
speaking to parents or grandparents. Always, of course,
their especially memorable remarks have been imbedded
in conversation, in the verbal give-and-take of life
as it takes place among severely harassed families.
And always, there have been responses, themselves
sometimes hard to put aside—a mother's proud sadness;
a father's stubborn struggle with despair; a grandpar-
ent's quiet, wry detachment; an uncle's stoic calm,
interrupted suddenly by an outburst of humor or
seething, only partially controlled indignation.

"I can't forget some of what I hear from patients,"
Dr. Williams wrote to me when I was working on my
college thesis and getting ready to go to medical school.
He added this qualification or afterthought: "even
after I've put some of their words into a poem." The
poem was his way of bringing the words together, sharp-
ening and polishing dozens and dozens of "raw
diamonds." Still, they cling to their original rough state
in one's mind; I suppose because they will always be
part of a human experience—something precious found

while doing a job. What follows in this book are a number of those rough diamonds, not given the larger, more enduring and important company of symbol, allusion, and metaphor that Dr. Williams could provide, but worth at least some little attention from readers who have an interest in the luminous moments of the lives of ordinary people. All I have done is listen, keep track of what I have heard with a tape recorder or by applying a pen to paper, and, later, extract the "red lollipops" from, sad to say, much that was all too drab, ugly, tasteless. (If that judgment risks being thought condescending and arrogant, it is nevertheless a risk that must be taken. Many of the people I have worked with have been not only poor but hungry, undernourished, badly sick, and subject to the indignities and humiliations that go with a lack of adequate or proper sanitation—the constant harassments of rats, flies, mosquitoes, bacteria, viruses, and even the absence of electricity.)

I wish to thank Paul Zimmer, poet and poetry editor of the University of Pittsburgh Press, for his constant encouragement and counsel; also, Frederick A. Hetzel, director of the Press, who has long been a friend—since the publication of a volume on the lives of migrant farm workers, based on my Horace Mann Lecture sponsored by Pitt. My wife's eyes and ears have always taken the measure of things before my own have been able to do so; a number of the spoken poems were heard as such by her, while I was grimly busy listening for content and making the analytic interpretations that seem to be an inescapable and unenviable fate for people like me. I am always grateful to Kirk Felsman and Bonnie Harris for treating with appropriate "medication" this particular writer's "illness." And to the memory of William Carlos Williams, as well as to the people I have worked with and learned from, I offer this book. "No ideas but in things," the New Jersey doctor said and said again, and asked us all to say and never forget. I think some of the men, women, and children I have come to work with have their own way of saying yes, indeed, to that prescription of the doctor's.

ONE

he words in this section tend to be soldiers. The time was the 1960s, and there were a lot of principalities and powers to take on. The listener was himself a marine of sorts—uptight, all too well trained in his widely celebrated profession. His ear had its obsessions and missed a lot of music. Moreover, those were often not days of celebration but, rather, of trial and agony acknowledged: the hectic and hectoring oratory of combatants, some of them surprised winners, some chronic losers familiar with hunger and desperately looking for a little food and drink. Their pleas and shouts, their fierce determination and wry, plaintive resignation, their pride and self-doubt supply a certain tone to the voices: the children and parents of the South, Appalachia, and our northern white and black ghettoes. For me there has been the task of editing, arranging, trimming, and extracting—the pulling together of comments scattered in the expanse of time spent with another person: what gets called these days (speaking of sad resignation!) a relationship.

RUBY'S DRAWINGS

Draw, make pictures,
Size up that strange doctor,
I think of him.
My own face, always strange
A missing eye in one drawing
A missing ear in another.
I don't know me
The mirror scares me,
The mob scares me.
I draw the white girl
whole, nothing missing anywhere.
When I draw a white girl
I know she'll be okay
I give her five fingers, five toes
I give her everything.
But with the colored
it's not so okay.
I try to give the colored
as even a chance as I can,
but that's not the way
it will end up being,
my crayons remind me.

TO GET THE PITCH

The first thing a black mother
has to do when her kids
play in the street
is teach them about the white man
and what he expects.
I've done it with seven
and two more to go.
My son says it takes time
to get the pitch.

My grandma says: "Sally
can get through those mobs,
she was born to and, one way
or another, she'll have to
do it for the rest of her life."

A black mother,
New Orleans, 1962

W H Y ?

Why would people want
to go beyond the swears and scare
and try outright to kill?
Why nothing better to do—
in the middle of night's watches,
except mind and hand busy
planting dynamite!

A Mississippi tenant farmer,
Greenwood, 1964

A HARD-PRAYING CHURCH

At a church in Atlanta,
a hard-praying one,
We're Baptists sometimes,
but sometimes we're
just ourselves.
We take the Bible at its word,
and goes off on our
own kind of original praying;
and lo, God speaks, says yes,
says that's right,
says keep talking,
says oh yes,
says don't stop talking, ever
to Me

UNPLEASANTNESS IN NEW ORLEANS, 1961

The homes a colored enclave
a sociologist said long ago.
Grandmother and grandchild
walking to school through
Spit and brandished fists,
through biceps tightened
tongues pointed, mouths filled
with what the black woman called
"unpleasantness"
pitilessly confronting them
with the need to make
terms with terror.
"I'd sooner die than show them
one ounce of fear
The worse it got the surer
I was we could outlast them."

WE HAS IT ROUGH

Us migrant workers
has it rough, but we knows
how to live with it,
we learned it so long ago
it's second nature, it's third nature.
It's only once—maybe,
once in a while things get bad,
so long as you keeps your wits
and doesn't ask for but your rights.

SELF-PORTRAIT

That's me and the Lord made me.
When I grow up my momma says
I may not like
how He made me,
But I must remember
that He did it,
and it's His idea.
So when I draw the Lord
He'll be a real big man.
He has to be, better be,
to explain about how things are.

A black girl of six
Mississippi, 1966

I T ' S   U P   T O   G O D

The children ask questions.
When they ask all the questions
they ask about color, too,
They see a white boy or girl
and they get to wondering
They want to know this and that,
and I don't know what.
I truly don't know what—
except the Lord likes everyone
because He makes everyone.
No matter what it's like around us
it's not the whole picture.
We don't make ourselves,
It's up to God,
He can fool us all.
At two or two and a half
I try to talk about God.
No one knows what color He is.
The Lord is a mighty big man.
I pray every day.
You know what I pray?
I pray the children
don't dislike themselves.
That's bad, not liking your very own self

A black mother,
Jackson, Mississippi, 1965

MY OWN PEOPLE

You see yourself and the white kids
and you find out the difference,
You say there is none
and if there is
You won't say what it be,
You just say it's my own people
and I can be proud of them,
even if it may turn out bad,
plenty bad.
But that's later,
You say that, too.

INSIDE, OUTSIDE

The teachers say it's inside,
all the trouble and the mean words
come from inside people with bad hearts.
But it's outside, too.
They're all the time outside the school
shouting at us

A black child of six,
New Orleans, 1960

ME, TOO

Me, too, white man me
I want peace and quiet
and to make my living.
Neither you nor I made
the world like it is.
Live and let live.
White man, are you so different
from the black all over the world?
There are a few rich
over you, white man
and me, too,
white man.
All I say is
Where do they really
give the black the little chance
the little white man gets—
New York? Boston?
Should I leave Alabama?

An Alabama sharecropper, 1968

K N O W   T O   B E   A F R A I D

It's like being two people.
Around here I'm just me,
going to school but downtown
I am another person,
"even in Atlanta" crossing
into white zones makes me change my step

Keep your fear of the white man,
my momma tells each of us
all the time until
we know it for ourselves.
Be afraid, be scared of being
curious, if you want to know
too much about them
you'll step too far,
you'll overstep.
Know to be afraid.

The ten-year-old son of a South Carolina-born sharecropper
who has moved to Atlanta, 1965

MOSTLY IT'S BURIED

It's like with cars and knives,
what's dangerous
and how to stay away from it
children either know or
won't live long.
They have to grow up scared of whites.
I make them store their fear,
lock it up in their bones
sneak it way inside
bury it, but know where
just in case.
The colored man he has to hide
what he feels
even from himself.

A black mother, Boston, 1974

S P E A K I N G

I'm not speaking for myself
I'm speaking for my children.
I'm speaking for Joseph and Sally and Harry
and Stevie and Benjie and Mary,
I'm speaking for them,
They enter my dreams,
in the night I see them grown older.
So I get the words out,
Do my complaining, hollering and
do my scolding
do my begging and pleading.
I'd better, don't you think.

A black mother, Boston, 1971

GROWING UP WITH LOVE

That's what my mother said:
Keep still from squabbling.
It's what I say to mine,
appreciate each other, I say.
A time to talk and argue
and a time to stop,
be glad we're here on earth.
There's a lot of love,
God's love and love of our kind,
if we could just sit
and *be* with each other

A black mother in a
Chicago tenement, 1970

L E T   U S   B E

Let us go
Let us be
Let us walk on our own,
with our own words,
not on the white man's stilts,
his words.
We have our own ways and dress
what we want, like,
what tastes good to us
our lives, our sweet time.

A black youth, Harlem, 1970

THE GODDAM STREET

I know her children,
have seen them getting ready
for what she calls
"the goddam street."
Each child has been held
and breast-fed in ways
well-nourished mothers might envy.
In the cold rat-infested flat
there is lively warmth
between mother and babies,
songs, smiles, sighs.
"I don't know how to do it,
how to keep my kids
from getting stained, ruined
I keep them close to me.
They can tell how much
I want for it to be good,
so, I hope they'll make it,
and I stop, say a prayer—
not expecting prayer to be
answered, not around here."

A   S O N G

Niggers, they're lower than our dog,
He knows his place
and I keep him clean.
They're dirty. Have you
ever seen the food they eat?
They eat pig food,
eat it just like pigs.
I'll be having breakfast
and I'll think of the niggers
eating theirs
anything they want
fat, they feed themselves fat
streak-o-lean they call it.
Can you imagine?

A member of a shouting white mob,
New Orleans, 1961

YOU FEEL FUNNY

We were as nerved up at first
as they were, the schoolrooms silent.
It was the first time
I ever knew a nigra
as a person,
It's strange how you feel funny
for a while; most kids
needed time to get used
to it—I mean to them

A white youth of sixteen, son
of a Georgia segregationist leader, 1964

I B E L I E V E

I believe God was
the one who led us here
He'd done it before,
asked people to move
across rivers and deserts.
I believe I hear God in church,
sometimes in the woods,
I'd hear his voice in the wind.
But in the city there's not much nature,
except us folks, a lot of people.
God has more on his shoulders
than us in Down Bottom Creek,
I believe that.
We can't go any place farther,
this is the last stop
before we meet Him.
In Chicago God isn't right at your side.

Clara, a mountaineer's wife
living in the city since 1967

DON'T EXPECT MUCH

I prayed, let me tell you I did,
my head all prayed out,
I thought God would say
the way to go is this way,
it'll be all right.
On the drive to Chicago
I said, Close your eyes,
don't look too hard,
don't expect much,
No rest in store for us
no guaranteed setup,
God looks after you in the *next* world.
Say good-bye to the mountains,
you know you'll either leave
or you'll near die of hunger, just about.

Now how can that trip go
for a man who loves
Down Bottom Creek and hates Chicago?
Better for my children up here.
Don't expect much, though.
I know my Bible, yes Sir,
I do. To my way of thinking
God suffered so we
wouldn't be the only ones.

A Kentucky mountaineer,
on the way to Chicago, 1970

TWO

*t*hese poems are another story, so to speak: the West, rather obviously; different people by far; and the visitor now on a somewhat altered mission. Even younger Pueblo and Hopi schoolchildren (say, those of seven or eight) have learned to be comfortable with an allusive, metaphorical, slyly suggestive mode of speech. They hint; often lacking bushes, they beat around inviting yet treacherous cacti. There is a dense, cryptic side to the conversations one hears on certain reservations of New Mexico and Arizona. And the itinerant observer, more significantly than ever away from the North-South that (from the distance of Albuquerque) amounts to the East, finds himself in no mood to poke or pry with questions meant to sidetrack people from what is on *their* minds.

Whatever "transcendence" is, I rather suspect it has been revealed to a number of Indians; but they have no desire to give a bill of particulars, to write the linear essays and books that would qualify them (in the eyes of others) as "philosophers," as knowing and thoughtful. ("Forgive us, Lord, the sin of sins, Pride.") The same holds for Eskimos—cleverly able to chatter, when smoke is necessary to distract sniffing dogs. What follows has been gathered over the years, fragments heard all over the (western and high northern) place— and put into one person's order and sequence: my sweaty, maybe grubby hand, their rather tasty morsels. Near the mesas of the Southwest or along the arctic coast "they" tend to be more than confused by the constantly proprietary nature of their visitors from the great beyond of the United States of America: who owns what?—the chant of the strong man. Words are a kind of property, and they belong to everyone in those Arctic villages or among the Hopis or Pueblos—even to a curious caller. Who wants to worry about someone's legal deed or table of measurements, when there is everyone's big yawn of a cottonwood tree down the road or, not far off, an ice floe that laughs at the sun, dares it to try its very best?

BLUE SKY

Blue Sky holding the Earth
Holding the sun, Chief of the bodies
Holding the stars, other worlds
Giving us the moon, night's bonus
Giving us air, our only chance
Sending us rain, our only chance
Sending us snow, a new chance
Talking to us:
The Wind shaking the trees
The Lightning points at the mountain
Thunder snaps its fingers, and we pay attention.

THE SPIRIT'S COVER

The sun gave us the sky
A blanket over the earth
Clouds came, running into races
Fights sometimes noise
Powwows the drums beating
Meetings, and then winners and losers
Accidents during the war
Spears of light thrown across the room
This room of ours
Under the Spirit's cover

THE MOON

The tired sun turns its back
The moon
The night smothers day's fire
The moon
The sun hurries elsewhere
The moon
The night makes itself at home
The moon
The sun bows, promises a return
The moon
The night arrives, says look at me
The moon.

T H E   V A L L E Y

My hands together a cup
The Valley holds us, even the birds
They go up, down, wing the edges
But stay. We stay
Anglos leave, cars crawling
Between all the fingers, motorcycles
Bragging their way through
Planes to the winds
Dust from the top
Of us.

THE SIGN

Wind the mesa whispers
Spirits upset or just playing
Balls of tumbleweed thrown down
The street a bowling alley
Anglos want numbers on doors
I walked across the desert
The ancestors nodded, a tree
Laughed, a bird
Teased, dust in my face
Stopped me, a rock caught
The feet, blood and a long look
The clouds smoky, the echo of shots
The Anglo sign: NO TRESPASSING

THE RIVER

Umpire, they are at you
Both sides the heavy-breathing
Bulls ready to charge red
Mexicans, the lost ones
On the other side of the watery tracks.
My people, the wandering beggars
Blood as divided as nations
The sun gives us its shadow
The Anglo giant drops pennies
Where are all of you
When we need you, now?
Great one, great river,
A name to honor
No exit one way—
But welcome wonderful visitors
Fiestas and silk scarves and water
For the dry mouths of tequila
Later you will slip across
Groping for your combs
Pinching your snow-white cheeks.
Mirror, mirror on the wall
Texas is the winner
Watch out you bloody umpire
Check your heart, mind your manners.

BLACK SKY

I

Black sky, sleep without dreams
The moon a big picture in the mind
Lights go on, action camera
They said on television
Black sky again between
Commercials they are everywhere
Stars come and say good-bye
Not for long, homesick
They are back flashing their messages
Saying I am here, forget me not
For Heaven's sake
Anglo flowers and our cacti.

II

Three years of army life
Three years of Morse code
The Signal Corps
And bodies before us to shoot
Make-believe in case of a war
Superstitious Indians, their crazy ideas
The stars wink, wonder at night
Where will the Anglos go next?
Is our turn coming soon?
One day we will stay asleep
Hiding all night, all day
Black sky, hunted big dipper
Holding little dipper tight.

A S P E N S

Lonely some near crawling cacti
Thin height a separate people
Others an army camped on hills.
Naked arms outstretched
Please spirits remember us
Give us our battle clothes.
Tossed green salad, a meal of thanks
The desert waits without envy
The mineral between animal and vegetable
The sun beats on us
It is New Mexico, no mercy
Fight fire with fire, we sing.
The leaves go to war
Orange and red march
The sun only blinks
Snow and our white fingers.

ADOBE

Up from the earth we came
Stopping only at the will of the gods
Those who take clay to hide.
The sun burns up centuries
In caves the mighty hug the dark
We say yes to the furnace
Throw away your thermometers,
Clever gods who stuff us full,
We will keep you cool
And take it, take it, take it
The sun making love to us.

THAT HORSE

That horse against the wall
The mesa against the sky.
That horse, rooted in the earth
The river's edge of cottonwood trees.
That horse grazing, dozing, never moving
The church on the distant hill
Looking us over
Yawning at our confessions
Giving no quarter to the Devil
Who rode on other horses.
There are seven nights
In everyone's week, the [liberal] primer says:
[Boasts] Anglos, Indians, the Spanish ones.

SPANISH BREAD

We are the old ones
Dough, rising growing bursting
Almost a ferment I start
But it is God's doing
I only sing to it.
Seventy years of dough
Seventy years of hands working at it
The words are inside
Outside, too: the butter.
I do not boast
The dough pulls my hands
My voice too. Sing!
Sí, I say *sí*, and begin
I feel the music in the bread
I eat the old songs
Words from the old country
Spanish words, Spanish bread.

Robert Coles

S U M M E R

A fog of mosquitoes turns
Red salmon pink, a row
Tanning itself, sweating to dryness
Summer's sun to hungry tongues.
The rage to breed, so little time
Plants huddle snatch the light
A *micro-climate,* runners
Probing the soil, seeds falling
With hope, but the child looks
Doubtful. The web-footed loon
Says beware with a cry that
Brings tears to the skimmed water.
Sled dogs dig in, the driving
Snow a fond memory
In July, Mosquito Month.
If only the wind would
Stop the torture, restore peace.

ALASKAN MEADOWS

Meadows meet the clouds
Light spreads fires on the tundra
Brown and gray to yellow and red
The frost leaves, sedges break through
The grasses push up, claim their green clothes
Hold each other tight: tussocks
Têtes de femme, the botanists
Also Alaskans tell Eskimo children
Who prefer bones covered with orange lichen
Who stalk foxes stalking lemmings.
The phalarope, the season's last brief visitor
Leaves the sea, dances on the ponds
Jabs for insects, eyes a *kayak*
A *umiak*, those larger vanishing birds.

CARIBOU TURF

Seeds sleep for centuries
Secrets of the barren slope
Fat everywhere, the birds
Fueled for flight, the squirrels
Ready to hide, the polar bear
Snorting and rolling with contempt.
The caribou once down to
Their last watery marrow
Lumber across the softened permafrost
Their turf. Pounds of back fat a reserve
Not vitamin chocolate seeds
But enough for a winter's
Arctic ecological expedition.

NUSHAGAK SLEEP

Antler bones, arms raised
Above the Nushagak hand, Death's friend.
The Eskimo said no, walked away
His canvas satchel full of meat.
We were left behind to tease the sea
Test the wind's will
Remind summer visitors to take care.
It is said we are a sanctuary
A stillborn child came to us
Plays us like a swing
One arm down, the other up
Tries to make us a raft.
But no, our horns have the arctic wind
To make lullabies, bring
The snow to tuck us in
Give us an infant's winter sleep.

A R C T I C   F A L L

The salmon bounding fall upon
Nets. The char strong plodders
Easily beat the rapids, but
Fail the waterfall's challenge, meet
The Eskimo's trap: *sapotit.*
Stone doors close, spears rush
To the defense of an Eskimo winter.
Meanwhile a scarlet robe for the tundra,
Bearberry leaves; and the smoky gold
Willows hang breathless from the earth
The lazy red mushrooms relax upon leafy beds
Above other beds of peat.
Berries signal the end, say
Come get us,
Forget your fishy stare
Touch us before the frost does
Eat our meat, the sweet red
Bilberry, the sour, black crowberry
Whose wings are the wind.

WINTER DARK

Spears of ice, the sun runs
Winter-dark in Alaska
Too many dreams
Too little food
The fish smile safe in the river
The Eskimo father carries his son
No empty hands, but the growl
A bear in the stomach
Ready, asking for blood.
None But the Lonely Heart
They played the schoolchildren
The white people who go weather mad here.

ICE   FLOE

Always here, even in summer
I soak up the sun, sweat
Dreams of better days.
They come with the wind
The birds wink at me:
So long to a winner.
The fish keep their distance:
Never trust someone who can't swim.
A polar bear struts all over me
Eyes all the time on the water
I move and am suddenly friendless
Why? Why the bear's good-bye?
Why the *kayak*'s shyness?
Even the snow gets restless
Leaves for the land
I turn to my mother
She laps me with love.

HUNGRY WINTER

Caribou once covered the land
Their feet thundered on the tundra
Their flesh a scent.
Sleeping dogs lie
Guards of still hungry Eskimos
Will the hungry winter eat us up?
Will the dogs prefer themselves?
The Lord's Last Supper
We pray to a white god
But we go to sleep singing
Our own lost, crying songs
Looking for the voices of the people.

E A R L Y   A R C T I C   L I G H T

The plane caught the beam
Their bird, a waitress in Fairbanks
She cannot think for herself.
Early light, touching restless huskies
Teams caught in the ropes
Near rocks eager to sparkle
Stars on the white sky
Wide leads cut through the shore
Of ice. The girl leaps
The dogs sniff stop short
She points upward
Her finger a gentle torch of first sun
And they follow.

NOORVIK SPRING

Fever of the first flowers
The surrendering snow
Islands of the sun's victory
The birds arrive, prepare: camouflage
The white winter hares carry
Black on their ears to prove their life
A single gull stands serene
Looks back toward its gray mantle.
Nets for the whitefish
Traps for the squirrels
The gun resting under the sun
The ptarmigan cock, defiant in his white summer
Watches the fateful spring come near.

Abba Kovner, *A Canopy in the Desert: Selected Poems*
Paul-Marie Lapointe, *The Terror of the Snows: Selected Poems*
Larry Levis, *Wrecking Crew*
Jim Lindsey, *In Lieu of Mecca*
Tom Lowenstein, tr., *Eskimo Poems from Canada and Greenland*
Archibald MacLeish, *The Great American Fourth of July Parade*
Peter Meinke, *The Night Train and the Golden Bird*
Judith Minty, *Lake Songs and Other Fears*
James Moore, *The New Body*
Carol Muske, *Camouflage*
Greg Pape, *Border Crossings*
Thomas Rabbitt, *Exile*
Belle Randall, *101 Different Ways of Playing Solitaire and Other Poems*
Ed Roberson, *Etai-Eken*
Ed Roberson, *When Thy King Is A Boy*
Eugene Ruggles, *The Lifeguard in the Snow*
Dennis Scott, *Uncle Time*
Herbert Scott, *Groceries*
Richard Shelton, *Of All the Dirty Words*
Richard Shelton, *The Tattooed Desert*
Richard Shelton, *You Can't Have Everything*
Gary Soto, *The Elements of San Joaquin*
David Steingass, *American Handbook*
David Steingass, *Body Compass*
Tomas Tranströmer, *Windows & Stones: Selected Poems*
Alberta T. Turner, *Learning to Count*
Alberta T. Turner, *Lid and Spoon*
Marc Weber, *48 Small Poems*
David P. Young, *Sweating Out the Winter*

The first edition of

A   FESTERING   SWEETNESS

consists of three thousand copies

in paper cover, fifteen hundred copies

hardbound in boards,

and fifty specially bound copies

numbered and signed by the author.